The Solar System

THE Sky

Núria Roca & Carol Isern
Rocio Bonilla

BARRON'S

The sky is spectacular

Alice and Oliver are looking at the sky. The Sun comes out early in the morning and the Moon appears at the end of the day.

"And when the sky is dark, it becomes filled with many little dots of light, which are the stars," says Oliver.

Looking very far away

Oliver sees a little dot moving high up in the sky, but he would like to see it better. Is it a planet? A star? A spaceship?

Alice explains to him that if they could go to an observatory, they would be able to look through a telescope, which is a tool that astronomers use to observe the sky.

Astronomy

Astronomers are people who study everything in the sky: the planets, the satellites, and the stars.

Astronomy is a very ancient science. There are many things in the sky, but the astronomers don't know them all yet!

The Earth is round

We used to think that the Earth was flat, but many years ago, we discovered that it is round! If you left your house and kept walking, you would eventually reach your house again, from the other side!

"We would be like two ants walking around a ball!" says Alice.

The Earth dances

The Earth is round and turns like a spinning top.
And at the same time, it revolves around the Sun!

It's like a dancer spinning as she dances around her partner, the Sun! That's why we say that the Earth is a planet. A planet is an astral body that revolves around a sun.

Let's travel!

The Earth is like a spaceship traveling through space. We are the passengers and, although we don't realize it, we also travel through space with it.

Space is very, very large, but the Earth never gets lost: It is always close to the Sun and always follows the same path.

The sky is not the same the whole year 'round

Things in the sky do not move in the same way. For example, in summer the Sun is higher in the sky, warms more, and stays out longer; in winter it is lower, heats less, and sets earlier.

Everything revolves around the Sun

The Earth turns like a spinning top and moves around the Sun. The Moon also turns and revolves around the Earth. There are also many neighboring planets that revolve around the Sun, too.

"Wait a minute, this is confusing! We don't understand anything!" say Oliver and Alice.

The Moon is always with us

"So, does the Moon rotate around the Earth?" asks Oliver.
"Exactly! The Moon is always with us!" says Alice's mother.

The objects that revolve around the Sun are called planets. Objects that revolve around planets are called satellites, such as a moon.

Day and night

If you turn and put your back to the Sun,
your belly is in the shade, right?

Well, this is what the Earth does to the Sun. As the Earth turns, the sunlight reaches one side, but not the other. And that is why we have day and night.

Why do we have winter?

"But that's not all. Imagine that the Earth had a head and feet. When the Earth turns with its feet pointing toward the Sun,

it is winter at the feet. Although the feet are closer to the Sun, the Sun's rays are less intense. At the same time, it is summer at the head. Although the head is farther from the Sun, the Sun's rays are more intense," says Alice's mother.

Where are stars when we can't see them?

During the day, we can't see the stars because the sunlight is so strong that it prevents us from seeing them. It's like trying to see the light from a flashlight on a sunny day.

At night, we can see the planets as well as the stars. "The stars sparkle, but planets don't," says Alice's mother.

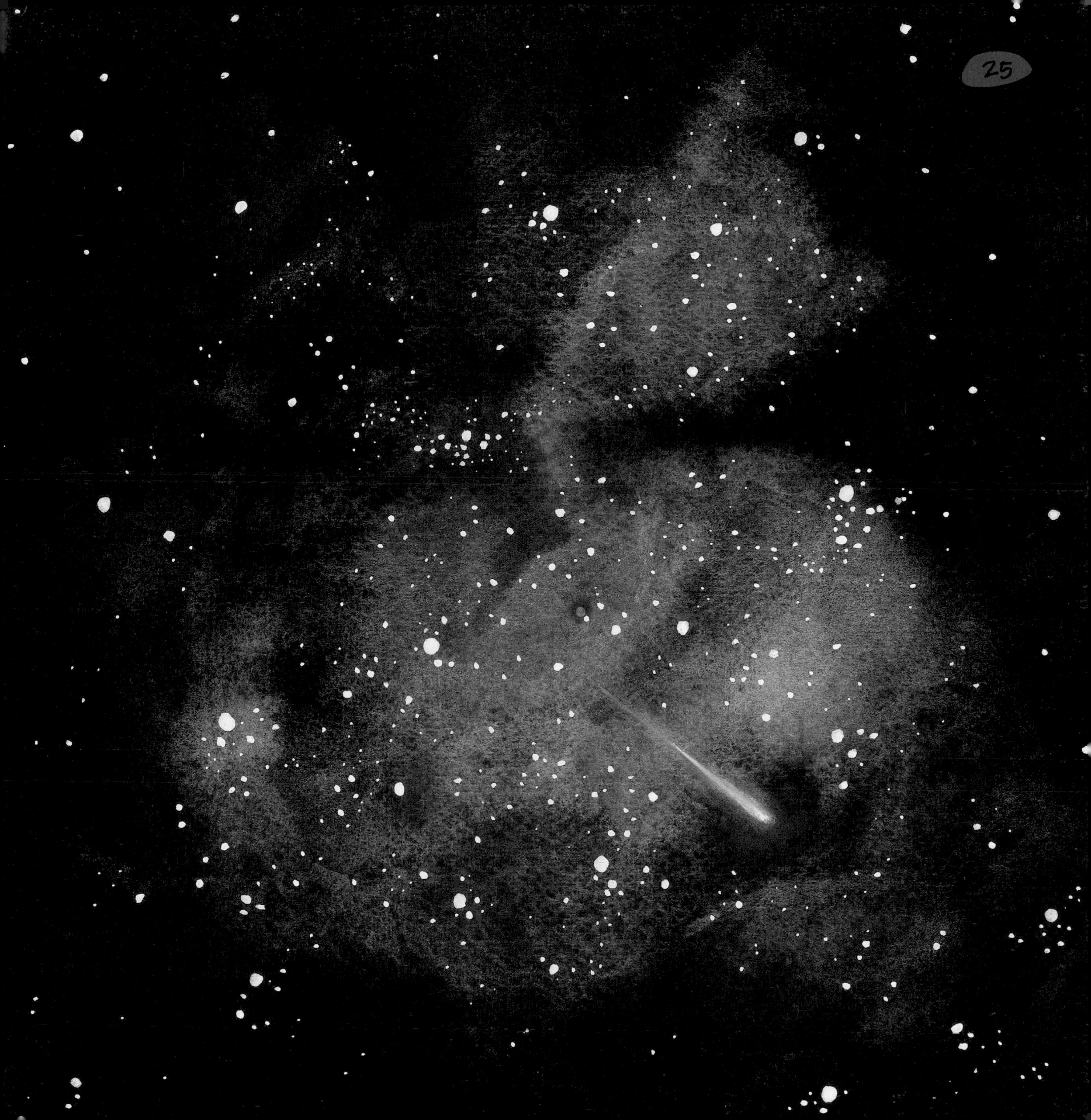

The solar system

Eight major planets revolve around the Sun: Mercury, Venus, Earth, Mars, Jupiter, Saturn, Uranus, and Neptune.

All of these, together with their satellites and other minor planets, form the solar system.

"I want to be the Sun because then the whole world would spin around me!" exclaims Oliver.

Stars

"And what about stars?" asks Oliver, who never tires of asking questions.

"No, stars do not revolve around the Sun. Stars are suns like ours, but they are much farther away than our sun," replies Alice's mother.

A space dance

Our solar system is made up of our sun and eight major planets that revolve around it.

This dance never stops... and it's always the same!
That's how we know when it will be winter and summer,
and when it will be day and night!

Activities

A trip to discover the distances between the planets

You can go on a trip to the countryside with Mom and Dad to discover the distances between the different planets. Take a tape measure with you and find a very open space. It doesn't need to be the size of a football field, but you must be able to run through it. Place a marble at one end of the field to represent the Sun and from there, measure: Mercury, 18 inches (45 cm); Venus, 32 inches (80 cm); Earth, 47 inches (120 cm); Mars, 71 inches (180 cm); Jupiter 20 feet (6 m). If you still have some space left, you can measure: Saturn 36 feet (11 m); Uranus 72 feet (22 m); and Neptune 115 feet (35 m).

Otherwise, just imagine the enormous distance there is between us and our neighbors!

Why do we have summer and winter?

Now we are going to do some craft work. You will need a lamp (such as a flexible table lamp), some modeling clay, a pencil (that you haven't sharpened yet) and an adult (could be Mom or Dad) to help you. With the modeling clay, make a large ball, at least the size of an adult's fist. When you have finished, stick the pencil through it so that it clearly emerges from the bottom part. Then place the ball, which represents the Earth, so that the lamp can shine on it with the pencil slightly diagonal. Look at how the light falls on it: Which zones are illuminated the most? If you move the Earth in a circle around the Sun (the lamp), you will see that inside the illuminated zone there is a lighter part and a darker part. In the darker part, it is winter because the light reaches it with less intensity, therefore, warms it less and it is colder. This means that the seasons change because the Earth changes its position in space in relation to the Sun.

An **astral body** has a specific form, for example: planets, satellites, stars, comets, asteroids, and meteorites.

A **telescope** is the main instrument used by an astronomer for research. It's like a gigantic magnifying glass used for seeing things that are very far away. Thanks to the telescope, astronomers can see the planets, the stars, the satellites, and everything that is in space.

Parent's guide

An **astronomer** is a scientist who studies the sky, the astral bodies, and all the phenomena that take place there, in other words, a scientist who studies astronomy. The astronomer observes the movements of the astral bodies, discovers new ones, and measures the distance between them.

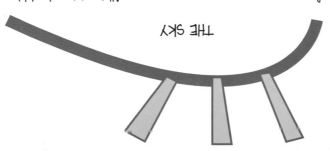

THE SKY

First edition for
North America published in 2014
by Barron's Educational Series, Inc.

© Gemser Publications, S.L. 2013
El Castell, 38 08329 Teià (Barcelona, Spain)
www.mercedesros.com
Text: Núria Roca and Carol Isern
Illustration: Rocio Bonilla
Design and layout: Estudi Guasch, S.L.

All inquiries should be addressed to:
Barron's Educational Series, Inc.
250 Wireless Boulevard
Hauppauge, NY 11788
www.barronseduc.com

ISBN: 978-1-4380-0477-8
Library of Congress Control Number: 2014935176

Date of Manufacture: June 2014
Manufactured by: L. Rex Printing Company Limited,
Dongguan City, Guangdong, China
Printed in China

9 8 7 6 5 4 3 2 1

During the day, the stars are not visible because the light of the Sun, the star in our solar system, prevents us from seeing the light from stars farther away. It's like trying to see the light from a flashlight in broad daylight on a sunlit terrace.

Proportionally, **the sizes of the astral bodies** in the solar system would be: The Sun, 1 m; Mercury, 3.5 mm; Venus, 9 mm; Earth, 10 mm; the Moon, 3 mm; Mars, 5 mm; Jupiter, 100 mm; Saturn, 80 mm; Uranus, 35 mm; Neptune is like Uranus, but slightly smaller.

Despite the fact that we see the Sun rise every day in the east and set in the west, and **it seems like the Sun is moving** from one end of the sky to the other, it is not moving, we are. It's like when you go on a rollercoaster: Things pass by very quickly before you, don't they? However, the things are not moving, we are.

A star is an astral body that has its own light, which makes it shine. A **planet** is an astral body that does not have its own light and revolves around a star (because in our solar system, the Sun is the star that gives us warmth and light), around which the eight planets revolve, one of which is the Earth. A **satellite** is an astral body that does not have its own light either and always revolves around another astral body, such as a planet.